Dedication

For my vibrant daughter,
Loren Olivia Rogers-Finch,
who fills my days with a
spectrum of joy,
and to my beloved Husband,
Richard Charles Rogers,
my steadfast co-pilot through
life's most beautiful journeys.

This book is also for our future
grandson, awaiting his grand
entrance, who already holds a
special place in our hearts and
dreams.

With Love always,
Kathleen Nansel Rogers

"A Smile is a Curve that sets everything Straight"-

Phyllis Diller

To:
_____

From: _____

Your thoughts are invaluable! If you find this book engaging, please consider leaving a brief review. Your feedback not only helps other readers discover this story, but also greatly supports my work. Thank you for taking a moment to share your experience.

A Little Note From Me, Kathleen Nansel Rogers

Hello there! This book is for you - whether you're just learning to walk or have been walking for many, many years!
While it's especially made for little ones
(around two and up), the happy secret inside - the amazing power of a smile - is something everyone needs to know, no matter how old they are.

The idea of this story sparkled in my mind because of my own life and all the wonderful art students I've taught over the past forty years. I noticed something special: so many children move and change schools quite a bit. I wanted to share something that could help make those changes a little easier.

When I started looking into what a simple smile can do, I was absolutely amazed! Even I learned so much as an adult. I really wish I had known these things when I was a child; it would have made such a big difference.
That's why I truly believe this book can be something special. Did you know that a little one starts smiling even before they're born, snuggled safe in their mother's tummy?
Smiling is something we all should keep doing our whole lives!
This isn't just a story; it's like a little helper, building up strength and happiness, one smile at a time. I hope it brings a little sunshine to your day.

Warmly,

Kathleen Nansel Rogers

Also by this Author:

Kathleen Nansel Rogers
My other Read Aloud Children's book on YouTube; Titled:
Mobar The Lonely Alien

https://youtu.be/0qN3LuFWFR0?feature=shared

Free on YouTube, this is a children's book, that teaches the importance of believing in yourself, trust is the basis of any relationship, fitting in takes time, and that you are not alone in your thoughts and feelings.

This book can also be used to educate adults as well as children, on the Nine Movie Guideposts, that all major motion picture movies follow, and knowing these guideposts, will make your movie watching experiences a much richer viewing.

It also teaches the six stages, that one needs to go through, to create an emotionally moving Art piece, taken from the world known: The Artist's magazine.

Teaching the importance of Descriptive Adjective's, to increase the feelings in a story. Introducing Mr. Fred Rogers quote; "Love is the root of everything in Life."

Also teaching that the more you see, the more you know, and the more you know, the richer your life will be.

The reading takes place from Mrs. Rogers Airbnb Listing, Clear Landing/Cabin in the Forest, in Christmas, Florida, where she has earned the much valued status as a Superhost!, Guests Favorite, and top 10%.

She introduces you to her two chicken's, (related to the King of Dinosaurs, T' Rex) named Buffy and Ziania. You are also shown her DIY creation of her book, made from a paper Grocery bag, with mediums of Elmer's glue, Black Acrylic paints, and Soft Pastels.

Also scope out my other books on Amazon.com: Books Here are my links:

Trust is the Basis of Any Relationship: Homer at Clear Landing: https://a.co/d/geVwXO1

Why Own a Dog: The Incredible Captain Buddy: How To Convince One To Buy a Dog: https://a.co/d/5uaLQhD

Hi Uncle "T": From The Chickee Chicks at Clear Landing: https://a.co/d/6ThRtBt

Airbnb Listing: airbnb.com/h/clearlanding-cabin-in-the-forest
Clear Landing/Cabin in The Forest
Christmas, Florida

Kathleen Nansel Rogers (b. Nov. 19, 1952, St. Louis suburb) is a prolific artist whose award-winning work, from childhood through nine accomplished shows, has inspired viewers globally. Her extensive education includes a B.A. (University of Central Florida), B.S. (Florida Atlantic University), Fort Lauderdale Art School, numerous workshops with 25 international instructors, and significant art coursework beyond her B.A., complemented by professional experience and near completion of a master's in psychology.

A dedicated educator for 40 years across all age levels, Rogers has guided over 10,000 students to win local, state, national, and international awards, including college scholarships. Her contributions earned her the FAMS Award and the National Teacher of Distinction Award.

Author of three previous 5-star rated books sold worldwide. Rogers art masterfully explores repetition in form, color, and shape. Her recent works integrate psychology, four-line expressions from the Elements of Art, the five basic shapes, and the Rule of Thirds to emphasize feelings, along with carefully selected color schemes to unify emotions evoked by songs, poems, quotes, or objects.

Throughout her distinguished career, Kathleen Rogers has exhibited in galleries and shows, including the King Performing Arts Center, leaving a significant mark on contemporary art. Her ability to blend diverse elements into cohesive narratives has established her as a respected artist.

Kathleen Nansel Rogers artistic journey reflects dedication, creativity, and commitment to innovation.

Her inspiring work continues to captivate audiences globally, fostering a shared appreciation for art's transformative power.

Copyright © [2025] by [Kathleen Nansel Rogers
Publisher Kathleen Nansel Rogers
All rights reserved.

This book is protected by copyright.
That means you can't copy or share any part of it without
special permission from the author or publisher,
except for vary small parts in a review.

LCCN: 2025906823

ISBN- 979-8-9985651-0-6 - Ingramspark - Hardcover

Once upon a time, nestled among rolling hills and vibrant trees - red maples, flowering dogwoods, wheeping cherries, and even delicious apple trees and juicy peaches - was a charming village.

A curious and adventurous boy named Oha (which means true knowledge) lived in this happy village. He loved how everyone's smiles made him feel. It was like sunshine wherever he went! He noticed that smiling was not just about being happy; it made people want to do their best and help others.

Sadly, Oha had to move away from his beloved village. His new town was ...different. No smiles. Everywhere he went, people looked glum. Oha missed the warmth and happiness of his old home. One day, Oha decided to be brave. He smiled at a stranger. And guess what? The stranger smiled back! It was not the big joyful smile that Oha was given, in his hometown, but it was a start. Oha kept smiling at people, and slowly, day by day, more people smiled back.

A smile can brighten your day and someone else's!
It makes you feel good and makes others want to be around you.
When you smile, good things often happen, leading to a happier life.
Smiling brings happiness!

True happiness starts inside. Take care of yourself by eating healthy foods, getting enough sleep, and...

exercising. When you feel good inside, it is easier to smile.

Smile when you watch animals. It is relaxing and makes you feel joyful, and you will see more.

Even squirrels notice a smile! Did you know squirrels are super smart? They remember people and will often pause to observe you if you offer a friendly smile. This will put a smile on your face, the next time that you see a squirrel bury a nut, keep watching, and you will see him go to another location, and pretend that he is burying another nut to trick his preditors!

This will also put a smile on your face. Squirrels also use their tails as a parachute when falling and whistle to other squirrels if there is danger, and more.

Do not be afraid to dance!
When you smile, your eyes light up,
making you feel more awake and alert.
Putting on a smile before you step onto the dance floor calms your nerves and creates a positive aura.
 If you delight in your movements and wear a smile, your mood will soar, and everyone watching will feel the joy radiating from you.
Dancing with a smile makes you happy and makes everyone around you happy too!

Drawing in a treehouse with a friend and a smile helps you connect with yourself and appreciate nature.

Explore the forest with a smile and you will see so much more! Nature is amazing.

Smiling while playing sports helps you perform better, called Strategic Gameplay! Professional athletes understand the power of smiling, and fans love to see their favorite playerssmiling, because they make the game look even more enjoyable!

You are special and precious,
like a jewel.
Take care of all parts of yourself -
your body, mind, and feelings.

Smiles Are FREE

So
Smile Smile Smile

Key Words to Remember to Smile for a Happier Life:

To: be your best, be friends, give yourself energy,

be brave, be a hero, look better, be strong, grow with others,

be true to yourself, be creative, have fun, take care of your brain,

care of your body, connect with animals, relax body and mind,

learn new things, sing better, get new ideas, improve self-control,

build motor skills, create critical thinking skills, enjoy dancing,

feel more awake, boost your mood, see things differently,

see more in life, sleep better, better remember, more focused,

feel hopeful, have a positive mindset, to score,

to win, called Strategic Gameplay,

have more fans, meet more people, build your emotions,

have a healthier heart, make everything true,

save yourself time, and to help others.

Smile Quiz

True (Yes) or False (No)

1.) Smiling gives you extra energy.
2.) Smiling helps give you new ideas.
3.) Smiling helps you to do your best.
4.) Smiling helps you to help others.
5.) Smiling helps you to be brave.
6.) Smiling helps you to be strong.
7.) Smiling helps you to be a hero.
8.) Smiling helps you to make friends.
9.) Smiling helps you keep trying.
10.) even if people are resistant.)
11.) Smiling will help make you happy.
12.) Smiling will help you grow with others.
13.) Smiling helps keep you from getting sick.
14.) Smiling will help you exercise.
15.) Smiling will help you to be creative.
16.) Will help you make friends with animals.
17.) Smiling while singing improves your voice.
18.) Smiling will help you to try new moves.
19.) Smiling improves critical thinking skills. (solving problems, making decisions).
20.) Smiling calms your nerves.
21.) Smiling helps you to see more.
22.) Smiling helps you to think more clearly.
23.) Smiling helps to relax you and learn more.
24.) Smiling encourages a hopeful outlook.
25.) Smiling improves brain functions.
26.) Smiling is a great Strategic Gameplay, to win in any activity.
27.) Smiling will help you to meet more people.
28.) (you learn something from everyone you meet, and every
29.) time you learn something, you make your life richer).
30.) Smiling improves your body, mind, and soul.
31.) Smiling helps keep you strong.

Smile Impact Quotes on Others

"Let us always meet each other with a smile, for the smile is the beginning of Love." -
Mother Teresa

"A smile is the light in your window that tells others that there is a caring, sharing person inside." - Denis Waitley

"Learn to smile at every situation. See it as an opportunity to prove your strength and ability." - Joe Brown

"A warm smile is the universal language of kindness." -
William Arthur Ward

"A simple smile reminds us of it's power to connect, heal, and uplift." -
Unknown

"The world always looks brighter from behind a smile." -Unknown
Smile! It increases your face value." - Robert Harling

"Share your smile with the world. It's a symbol of friendship and peace." -
Christine Brinkley

www.ingramcontent.com/pod-product-compliance
Lightning Source LLC
Chambersburg PA
CBHW051326110526
44582CB00003B/61